Louth

in old picture postcards volume 2

by
David Cuppleditch

European Library - Zaltbommel/Netherlands MCMLXXXVI

Cover picture:
Composite view of Louth, which includes the town's coat of arms and motto 'Deo Adjuvante Non Timendum'. Roughly translated 'With God's assistance there is nothing to fear'.

In preparing this volume I would like to thank Norman Cawkwell, Charles Smith, Mary Duke, Chris Birchmore, Mrs. Cottam, James Baildom Esq., Richard Mawer and Mrs. Gipps, for lending me certain postcards. Also a special thanks once again to Ken Atterby and indeed anyone whom I may have inadvertantly forgotten, who has helped to make this publication possible.

Since I dedicated volume one to my mother I am obliged to dedicate volume two to my father who has done much to promote Louth's well-being over the years.

GB   ISBN 90 288 3369 2 / CIP

© 1986 European Library - Zaltbommel/Netherlands

European Library in Zaltbommel/Netherlands publishes among other things the following series:

IN OLD PICTURE POSTCARDS *is a series of books which sets out to show what a particular place looked like and what life was like in Victorian and Edwardian times. A book about virtually every town in the United Kingdom is to be published in this series. By the end of this year about 300 different volumes will have appeared. 1,500 books have already been published devoted to the Netherlands with the title* **In oude ansichten.** *In Germany, Austria and Switzerland 650, 100 and 25 books have been published as* **In alten Ansichten;** *in France by the name* **En cartes postales anciennes** *and in Belgium as* **In oude prentkaarten** *and/or* **En cartes postales anciennes** *150 respectively 400 volumes have been published.*

For further particulars about published or forthcoming books, apply to your bookseller or direct to the publisher.

This edition has been printed and bound by Grafisch Bedrijf De Steigerpoort in Zaltbommel/Netherlands.

INTRODUCTION

Sequels are not usually a good idea but the publishers were so overwhelmed with the response to 'Louth in old picture postcards' volume one, that they have asked me to compile a companion to it. As such I have tried to concentrate on the more unusual aspects of the town; Louth hides a multitude of secrets and its peculiarities are often forgotten or simply overlooked. That the town has changed enormously may not at first be apparent but on closer inspection it has clearly altered considerably. Largely due to astute businessmen and eager property developers many buildings have been demolished or adulterated. Fortunately there is a core of loyal Ludensians who keep battling against the onslaught of enthusiastic builders and unscrupulous speculators.

In attempting to assemble this set of old postcards not only have I tried to show how the town has developed but have also featured some of the characters who have added to its 'flavour'. Moreover, this is not a history but instead a few notes strung together in response to the fascination of these old pictures. The trouble with local history is the more you delve into it, the more absorbing it becomes and in this slim volume I have only been able to capture snatches of what life has been like over the past hundred years. Nostalgia is in fashion at the moment and so this little book along with its companion volume will have its place amongst Louth's comprehensive set of literature. The town is still expanding so I hope that these postcards will serve to help the younger generation understand their heritage.

Over the years many famous people have visited Louth. Lloyd George was quite captivated by the town and offered every assistance when he heard about the 1920 flood. Another surprising guest was the young Mahatma Gandhi who stayed with Billy Ashley and his sisters at 12 George Street for some two weeks or so. The late Jack Smith who was taxi driver at the Masons Arms remembered driving Gandhi in a horse and carriage from Louth station to George Street and also that he wore a dark blue suit and not the usual costume which we normaly associate with that great Indian leader. In times gone by Lord Byron was reputed to have stayed at the Manor House in Eastgate and Cromwell in the old 'Horse and Jockey' on the corner of Upgate with Mercer Row now known as 'Cromwell House'. Incidentally the Byron connection with Lincolnshire does not end here because his bookcase (a large ornate and impressive piece of furniture) now lies in Locksley Hall, North Somercotes. Other noteable visitors to the town have included, General Booth, of the Salvation Army, who paid a flying visit; General Baden Powell; John Betjeman (the late poet Laureate and great friend of Jack Yates). More recently sports personalities such as Geoff Capes (the Lincolnshire policeman and Olympic shot putter), 'Hurricane' Higgins (the enigmatic snooker player), and Buster Mottram (the up and coming tennis player) have all visited Louth. In television too an episode of 'Nanny' with Wendy Craig in the title role was filmed in the Cornmarket.

But Louth does not just attract the famous and well-known. Part of its charm is that Louth attracts characters from all walks of life. One such individual was a midget. There were two midgets who could be seen in the town in the 1950's and 1960's. They both looked very similar; one was called John Lusby and the other Cyril Holland. As boys we nicknamed John Lusby 'Big Pete'. On reflection this seems a bit cruel, but at the time it was quite appropriate. 'They're coming over in planeloads!' Big Pete would say, 'Who?' we would ask. 'Foreigners,' he would retort. A truly prophetic statement for those days. 'Where are they coming from?' we would ask innocently. 'From Horncastle, Sleaford, Grimsby and Skegness!' was Big Pete's reply.

No matter how many books are written on Louth and I hope there are many more, each one will add a new insight into the development of what was once a wool town and is still a thriving community. Since writing 'Louth in old picture postcards' volume 1, Mr. Benton's erudite 'Louth in Early Days' has appeared and I know a number of others are planned; but it is one thing to plan a book and quite another to sit down and write it.

Perhaps one day we will see more books of this nature appearing more frequently because I feel the definitive history of Louth has yet to be written.

LOUTH Parish Church.

Rev. CANON WILDE, M.A.

1. Daniel Defoe once said that Louth was 'famous for a fine spire steeple' and undoubtedly St. James Church spire is the towns greatest asset. It is the tallest parish church spire in the country and not only dominates the town but also the surrounding area for miles. This card was produced when Canon Wilde was Rector of St. James.

Louth Market Place in 1865.

2. In this next card of the market place one of the earliest Louth photographs was used. Despite the date (1865) it would not have been used as a postcard until 1895. Depicting a quaint row of shops which were demolished by those 'dreadful Victorians' in preparation for their new market hall, it shows the damage which can be done by developers. I doubt whether conservationists would have approved of a similar scheme these days and quite rightly.

3. On the corner of the market place stood Emerson's fruit, vegetables and poultry stores. Game of every description hung from poles outside the shop, but isn't that old gas lamp a beauty? When I was a boy this shop was simply known as Strawsons, selling fruit and vegetables.

4. This is not the boys in the back room but rather the girls in the cutting room of Eve and Ranshaw's or at least some of them. A large prestigious draper would think nothing of employing anything up to twenty people at a time to cut, alter and make bespoke tailoring.

Elkington Hall **Louth,** *Lincs.* W. G. SMYTH.

Chas. Parker, Market Place, Louth.

5. Louth has acted as a centre to a wide circle of villages and large houses, for example Elkington Hall. This postcard (produced by Parkers) depicts an early photograph of Captain Smyth imposed on a view of the Hall which has since been demolished.

6. In this next card dated 1900 (Christmas day and taken at Elkington Grange) a much older Captain and Mrs. Smyth are seated in the centre of this family gathering. I like the Victorian fez which the venerable old captain is wearing. The Reverend Smyth can be seen here standing in the middle of the group and although it was fashionable to have large families in Victorian times, most of this entourage seems to be made up of clergymen and maiden aunts.

Photo by Hickingbottom & Bullamore, **Elkington Hall, from Lake, near Louth.** *Lincoln.*

7. Yet another view of the Hall, this time from the lake. It was one of a pair of cards produced by Hickingbottom and Bullamore of Lincoln. During the Second World War Elkington Hall was the home of Lord Wilton. The Dobsons were the last family to live here before the house was knocked to the ground.

WALMSGATE.

190

8. Another important house with Louth connections was Walmsgate Hall. Formerly the home of the Dallas Yorkes and latterly Mr. and Mrs. Haggis this fine mansion has also, sadly, been demolished. It was here that the beautiful Winifred Dallas Yorke, later to become the forth Duchess of Portland, was born. One saving grace about Walmsgate is the small chapel which used to stand near to the hall. The contents and pieces of the interior were removed before it was demolished and taken to Langworth, near Lincoln where they can be seen today.

TATHWELL, LOUTH.

9. Nearby villages and hamlets which looked to Louth were Tathwell, Burwell, Fulstow, Legbourne, Covenham, Alvingham, Cockerington, Fotherby, Grimoldby and Cawthorpe. In fact I would go so far as to say that all the immediate area considered Louth as its shopping centre and general meeting place. Tathwell, for example, was a quiet sleepy place. Only a certain section of its community could afford horses and carriages which meant the rest of the residents had to travel on ponies and carts or walk to town on market day. This postcard is of Tathwell village.

River Head, Louth.

10. Just as Louth serviced its neighbouring villages so the town was served by rail and canal. These lifelines kept a constant supply of foodstuffs and essential goods flowing through the town. This view of the riverhead shows some of the wharfs and warehouses which lined the canal storing many hundreds of tons. In fact the riverhead became a little village all on its own.

11. Over the years Hubbards Hills has done some sterling service for the town not only has it provided a pleasant refuge for Ludensians to walk their dogs or simply look at the scenery but it has also become a popular tourist venue attracting visitors from all over the county. This early card was produced by Jackson's of Grimsby.

12. The course of the river has altered many times and many fallen trees have touched the hearts of succeeding generations but the beauty remains the same. In autumn when few people walk the hills this must rank as one of the most peaceful and attractive spots in Britain. In this postcard which is reminiscent of Tennyson's Brook the tree on the right has since been felled only to be replaced by a scion.

13. Strangely enough informal Edwardian snapshots of friends or loved ones walking in the Hills are rare. Here is an exception depicting a young swell sporting a handsome moustache and boater and looking like an officer recently risen from the ranks. Posing as Jerome K. Jerome's 'the Idler' with cigarette in hand and watch chain dangling, the onlooker in the background is obviously fascinated by the spectacle.

Rustic Shelter,
Hubbard's Hill, Louth

14. One of the few remnants left in the Hills from the years before the First World War was this Hubbards Hills shelter. It stood until 1985 when under the weight of graffiti, vandalism and general weathering it was pulled down. Fortunately the hut which has replaced it is almost a carbon copy and East Lindsey District Council should be congratulated for taking the time and care to produce such an accurate replica.

THE OLD PAPER MILL, LOUTH

15. The River Lud once had thirteen working mills according to the Domesday Book in 1086. Now it only has one and that at Alvingham which has been patiently renovated to working order by Mr. and Mrs. Davies. The Wheel at Thorpe Hall mill seen here stopped turning many years ago. Since then it has been a trout farm and has now been converted into luxury homes.

N. SOMERÇOTES
UNIONIST CLUB

MRS BRACKENBURY LAYING FOUNDATION STONE

16. Mrs. Brackenbury, wife of the Conservative M.P. for Louth, who lived at Thorpe Hall, is seen here laying the foundation stone at the Unionist Club, North Somercotes on 6th July 1911. (A picture of Thorpe Hall appeared in volume one.) Brackenbury toppled Perks (the Liberal M.P.) and started a long line of conservative M.P.'s in this century who included: Col. Heneage, Cyril Osbourne, Jeffrey Archer (the novelist), Michael Brotherton and currently Sir Peter Tapsell.

St. Mary's Road, Louth

17. Just around the corner is St. Mary's Lane. For some unknown reason it was called St. Mary's Road on this postcard but undoubtedly the lane was named after St. Mary's Church (situated on or near the old cemetery). Depicting some highly desirable Edwardian villas. These dwellings sold quickly and have been much sought after ever since.

18. At this point I was hoping to include some post-cards commemorating the Ladies verses Gents cricket match of 1902 but unfortunately the cards were so faded that reproduction proved impossible. So instead I have included a photo of 'Snacker', who played for Louth Cricket Team, which was probably more enthusiastic than professional. This photo was taken on the London Road sports ground, in the days of gentlemen players.

Grimsby Road, Louth

19. Looking down the Grimsby Road towards Louth the view has hardly changed at all. That is apart from the attractive Edwardian Bridge which once spanned the road from Hollowgate on one side to its garden on the other. Now the residence of Mr. and Mrs. Lomas, I can remember it as the home of the Sandwith family who lived here for many years.

20. The bridge (once a feature of the town) was erected in 1907 by Matthew Jackson. Seen here standing on the bridge Matthew Jackson was a successful corn merchant, whose son Sydney took over the business and also became Mayor of Louth in 1918/19 and 1925/26.

21. In those halcyon days before the First World War three charming old ladies sat for their photograph in the garden of Hollowgate. Taken in the summer of 1910 the ladies who were dressed in their best Sunday bonnets were, from left to right: Mrs. Emma Wright of Eastfield Road, Mrs. Dennis and Miss Harriet Jackson, who was housekeeper for Mr. Samuel of Mount St. Mary's.

22. There has long been a house on this site and it may even have been the original vicarage of St. Mary's Church. Certainly part of St. Mary's graveyard overlapped into the garden of Mount St. Mary's. I shall always remember it as the home of the Nicholson family (Dr. Nicholson was a well-respected surgeon at Louth County Hospital). Other owners in the twentieth century have included Mr. Samuel (the clock maker), the Reverend Honey, Mr. Rushforth, Dr. Laughton-Smith and at present Mr. and Mrs. McFarland.

KEDDINGTON

23. One of the most neglected parts of Louth is Keddington which has a pretty little church and is a quiet and peaceful residential area. Andreas Kalvos, the Greek poet (1792-1869), was buried in the churchyard until 1960 when the bodies of Kalvos and his wife were exhumed, flown to Greece and reinterred in the poets birthplace of Zante. This underated poet spent about fourteen years of his life in Louth while his English wife ran a ladies boarding school in the town. (Jack Yates, the writer, is also buried in Keddington churchyard.) At the time this photograph was taken the charming thatched house (on the left of the card) belonged to the Sharpley family.

THE HIGH HOLME, LOUTH.

24. Another overlooked part of Louth is High Holme Road. This magnificent building, situated next to the County Hospital, was in fact two separate houses. Mrs. Huddlestone lived in one whilst Mrs. Langdale lived in the other; then it became a nurses home before being demolished altogether and the site is now a car park.

25. A bit further along High Holme Road, this delightful picture of Louth fire engine was taken. Frank Cottam who worked at Thorn's Livery Stables is riding the front horse and the old malt kiln (in the right of the photo) is clearly visible in the background. Mind you, the whole scene looks very odd in this picture because we have become so accustomed to the houses which are built there now.

26. The trouble with old postcards and especially photographic views is that eventually they will fade. This view of South Street is a particularly good example. In another few years the image on this card will have gone altogether. In fact South Street has changed little in the last 80 years, some of the foliage may have gone and the wrought iron railings went in the war effort but the buildings are still much the same and it remains a narrow street especially for the amount of traffic it now has to cope with.

27. Over the years Louth has been served well by that august body known as the G.P.O. This photograph was taken circa 1905 by A. James when the post office was situated in the Market Place on the site now occupied by the Bakers Oven, next to the International Stores. Postmaster Reed (6th from the left, front row) was in charge and the postmen who can be identified are, back row (right to left): Rawlings, Ruffel Ward, Z. Gowing, Bell, J. Barton, Johnson, Hempstock, P. Mee plus three others; centre row: Catchpole, an unknown postman, Warne, Patrick, another unknown postman, T. Auested, Clark, Erriman, Goodall plus one other; front row: another unknown postman, Wilson, Brewer, Mrs. Blakey, Carter, postmaster Reed, Wilson, yet another unknown postman, Whitworth (who became postmaster at Windsor), Donner and Borman.

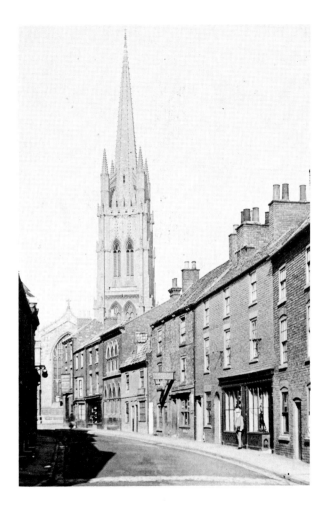

28. In its heyday this was the view looking up Little Eastgate towards St. James Church, before the present post office had been built. Dated at roughly the same time as the last photograph this postcard shows what Little Eastgate looked like before the many alterations of recent times.

29. In reverse, this was the view of Little Eastgate from the spire of St. James. Showing a panoramic view of the town including the new post office being built in 1930.

30. This charming portrait study of dentist James Goy, complete with Victorian frock coat, was taken in about 1875 by the celebrated Lincoln photographer Slingsby. Mr. Goy had moved his dental surgery to Shamrock House in Ramsgate, Louth from Lincoln. (A picture of Shamrock House appeared in volume 1.)

31. It would seem that James Goy encouraged youthful activities from the faint lettering on this card. Referring to this army of young ragamuffins and urchins assembled in Alexandra Road (just behind the Almshouses), it says 'Councillor Goy's Army'.

32. Just around the corner was the firm of A.W. Jaines, furniture remover and haulage contractor. Their offices were based at 11 Maiden Row which is known today as Church Street. This photograph was taken nearby in Ramsgate with the United Reformed Chapel in the background and Edward Garland's photography shop to the extreme right. Garland's photography shop was later taken over by Clare and after its demise as a photographic premises became an electricians store room before being demolished and the site now houses public conveniences.

33. At about the same time this row of terraced Victorian houses was built. They were named after the Reverend Orme who put up much of the money for the almshouses just opposite. Fortunately the Fine Fare supermarket complex which has just been erected to the right of these buildings, blends in well.

34. This view of Padehole (now called Northgate) shows the back entrance to the Pack Horse Tavern and also the pediment of the Northgate Primitive Methodist Chapel. On the left is Albert Horsewood's old antique shop and premises (now Chic's the plumber). These buildings were once used as the cabinet works of the Eve family (latterly the firm was known as Eve and Ranshaw) who gave their name to Eve Street.

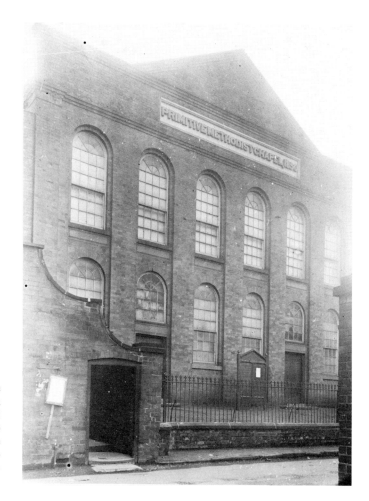

35. No this is not the Wesleyan Chapel in Little Eastgate but the Primitive Methodist Chapel in Northgate. Built in 1850 it stood as a chapel until the Second World War when it was converted into Pickford's warehouse. Then in the mid-1970's the roof caved in, due to neglect, and the entire building had to be demolished. (The door to the extreme left led to a Sunday school.)

36. It is difficult to believe that only eighty years ago women of all classes would not dare to enter a pub unless they either owned the premises or served there. Moreover the licencing laws were so flexible that anyone could drink anywhere at any time of the day or night (this was before the First World War restrictions). In 1869 at a special meeting of the Louth Borough Council it was decreed that all pubs in the town should close between 1 am and 4 am after the council had heard a petition from angry residents who were presumably fed up of being kept awake by rowdy revellers. 'The Brown Cow' public house on Newmarket was a respectable hostelry at the turn of the century. It had mixed fortunes and by the 1960's was rather run down. Completely renovated and revived by the Smith family it now enjoys a new lease of life as 'The Newmarket Inn'.

37. Next door to the Brown Cow was this peculiar building which was simply a one up one down terraced house. The beauty of Louth is that these odd buildings appear from time to time just to break the monotony of uniform terraces. The last occupant of this house was Mr. Goodwin.

38. Mr. Baildom started his removal firm and furniture store in 1876 in a small shop opposite the Fish Shambles. By the turn of the century the firm had expanded so much that larger premises were needed and so he moved to 127 Eastgate. The company remained there until 1955 when Baildom's ceased trading altogether. The shop is still a furniture store today, known as 'Times Furnishing' and luckily the ornate initials of J.B. carved so beautifully on the doors, have been retained.

39. This was a Mayoral procession walking through the town at the turn of the century (the tradition is still continued today). What is interesting about this postcard is the firm of L. Mayer & Son at 112 Eastgate, next door to Kelly's General Supply Stores. Mayer's butchers boasted the best House in Louth for home cured hams and bacon and were responsible for the famous 'Lindsey' pork pie.

40. No one did more to propagate literacy in the town than John William Goulding (1844-1922), printer and bookseller. This informal snapshot was taken in the garden of 28 Gospelgate. When he died his daughters continued the business until it was taken over by Jack Yates and eventually closed circa 1960.

Mercer Row, Louth

41. Goulding's bookshop (halfway down the left hand side of Mercer Row) blended in nicely with the other businesses in what was considered Louth's main thoroughfare. Mawers the butchers on the immediate left and Henry Forman's restaurant and bakery in Upgate (just visible in the distance) have gone, but Larder's shop which has changed remarkably little over the years still thrives as a successful grocery store.

Lincs. Show, 1909. Louth Market Place.

42. In the years up to the First World War, Louth enjoyed a brief respite of well-ordered functions such as the Lincolnshire show of 1909. I have often wondered what happened to the old pump which stood in the foreground but no one seems to know.

43. Even on Empire Day held in the same year there was much youthful enthusiasm and although the country was well-prepared no one wanted to think of war.

LOUTH CAMP JULY 1910 PB 220

44. However, in this next card taken in July 1910 there were more ominous overtones of what was to come.

LOUTH CAMP JULY 1910. P. B. 15

45. Yet with typical Lincolnshire aplomb you can almost hear the jokes and ribald comments coming out of Louth Camp.

East Gate, Louth

46. Just before the Great War (1914-1918) this was the view looking up Eastgate and although the business names have changed it is much the same these days. Apart from Cheetham's Store on the right hand side which was converted into the electric Picture Palace in 1914. It ran for nearly fifty years as a prosperous cinema, although later known simply as 'The Palace'. It closed in the late 1950's and was converted into a supermarket.

Ramsgate

Alms Houses, Louth.

Eastgate

47. After the First World War Louth returned to normality. This was the view at the junction of Ramsgate with Eastgate before the War Memorial was built.

48. There have been two monumental events in Louth's history to effect the whole country. The first was the Lincolnshire Uprising of 1536 which was sparked off when two of Cromwell's men came to take over the nunnery at Legbourne. The Abbess was held in such high esteem by local people that they were insensed by this action. With the fear that the same fate would befall St. James' Church and encouraged by the local Vicar practically the entire town took up arms and were ready to march to London. Fortunately they only reached Lincoln before dispersing. All that is left today of Legbourne Abbey are the foundation stones in the grounds of its fifty acre estate. This postcard circa 1910 was taken after extensive Edwardian refurbishments. Prior to that the building was a farmhouse with many outhouses and farm buildings. The Hall family lived here from 1937 to 1980 when it was bought by Mr. and Mrs. Morton.

THE LOUTH DISASTER. MAY 29TH 1920.   No 7.

W. BENTON.
52 RYE HILL.
NEWCASTLE
ON TYNE.

49. The second event to affect the whole country was the 1920 Louth flood.

W.BENTON.
82 RYE HILL
NEWCASTLE
ON TYNE.

THE LOUTH DISASTER MAY 29TH 1920. Nº 12.

50. Few other disasters can have been quite so well-recorded as the Louth flood. There were well over a hundred views recording the event from the media of the time, which inevitably poses the question – were the profits from these postcards donated to Louth flood victims? Or was it simply a case of photographers and media men cashing in on a tragic episode?

51. It is odd how the British stick together in times of disaster. Shortly after the flood crateloads of fish were sent from Grimsby, blankets arrived and an appeal fund was set up. Although the flood happened on 29th May 1920 by 2nd June the Mayors relief fund had reached £5,000. (The Mayor was Councillor Lacey.)

THE LOUTH DISASTER. MAY 29TH 1920. No. 5.

52. After the flooding, mopping up operations began. This postcard (one of a series) was produced by Mr. W. Benton of Newcastle on Tyne and indeed Benton's postcards were the best.

53. This was the view looking up James Street with what is now the WEA headquarters on the left hand side.

Brickyard back of Eve St

54. The damage to Louth was extensive as can be seen in this brickyard which was situated just behind Eve Street. Many vehicles were damaged beyond repair, this lorry (a vehicle of some considerable weight) had simply been overturned by the onrush of water. One car which was lost in the flood was never found at all.

The Louth Disaster, May 29th. 1920.
Jam of Barges at River Head.

34

W. Benton
82 Rye Hill
Newcastle on Tyne.

55. The riverhead took a bashing too, splaying barges and small boats all over the place.

Within the image: W.BENTON. 82 RYE HILL NEWCASTLE ON TYNE.

THE LOUTH DISASTER. MAY 29TH 1920. Nº 10

56. Yet another Benton postcard of Ramsgate. The Trinity Social Institute (it was also used as an occasional schoolroom) on the right hand side of this postcard was completely wrecked.

57. Looking at the devastation that was caused, it is no wonder that few Ludensians like to recall this tragic episode. The interesting thing about this postcard is not so much the people as the assortment of possessions which are piled high in the street and which housewives are so desperately trying to salvage.

58. This group shot was taken in the municipal car park next to the British Legion Hall in Northgate. The old rifle range is the long narrow building in the background. Sergeant Rowarth (the jovial soldier leaning against the cannon) is recogniseable as indeed is 'Tommy' Blyth (the gentleman with the boater) who is doling out the fish to needy victims.

59. At the funeral service Canon Lenton presided. The Berry family lost three children. Their hearse was drawn by a white pony and was embowered with flowers. During the flood Mrs. George Berry had desperately tried to save two of her three children by hanging them on meat hooks from the ceiling and balancing them on cupboards.

60. In this card we see a gaping great hole through a group of terraced houses in Ramsgate, which shows that many people lost their homes altogether. The only reminder of the flood these days are a few tide marks about the town to show the water level and a sinister grey obelisk made of Aberdeen granite which was unveiled by Dr. Stanley Walker on Saturday 2nd June 1923 in Louth cemetery.

61. One of the saddest sights in Louth today is Crowtree Lane Hospital. Built and paid for by the good people of Louth at a time when the town sorely needed a hospital, it now stands derelict and forlorn. The building was handed over to the N.H.S., by the trustees in 1948 and its fate now rests with indifferent bureaucracy.

62. Every year there was a charity event to raise money for the hospital. Because it was independant all funding had to come from donations and local subscription. There was a parade with floats which went through the town and the day ended on the London Road sports ground with a football match. This snapshot and the following postcard were taken in 1923.

63. To show the sort of local support which the hospital enjoyed this is yet another view of Mercer Row showing the crowd of people on their way to the event. What is noticeable in the melee is the number of cloth caps.

64. One of the floats which won a first prize in the parade was 'Banana Bob's' entry. This was an old Wright's bus adapted to fit 'Banana Bob's' needs both as a stall and as a conveyance. He collected most of his produce from Hull docks in this wagon and could be found on the fish shambles on Wednesdays, Fridays and Saturdays.

65. On 14th June 1927 Princess Helena Victoria opened the new wing of Crowtree Lane Hospital. It was built by Mawer Bros. and the new extention included a maternity unit, an X-ray department, a nurses home and a new children's ward.

66. In 1930 a year after Monk's Dyke school had opened there was a prize giving. Assembled here from right to left are the Reverend William Hind, Mr. Pridmore (the tailor), Mr. Lacey, Mrs. Lacey, Mr. Parker, Mr. John Coney, Percy Latter, an eager young journalist and Charlie Cheeseman (in blazer and cricket whites). Probably the most famous old boy of Monk's Dyke school is Donald Pleasence, the actor.

Eastgate, Louth

67. During this time it was safe to walk the streets of Louth. There was little traffic because few people had cars. Even as late as the 1950's there were few vehicles to block the middle of town and so no need for parking restrictions or organised car parks. Container traffic was unheard of, as the railway took care of heavy goods. This was the view looking up Eastgate. Most of the other familiar names such as Carter Walton and the Jolly Sailor have gone although C.R. Laking (the sign just under the clock) still operate their successful butchery business in Little Eastgate.

68. Of all the photographs taken in the town hall this one is perhaps the most nostalgic. Taken in the council chamber in 1932/33 the group are, from left to right: back row, Mr. Efemey, Dr. Laughton-Smith, Mr. Ingram, Mrs. Price, Arthur Price, Mr. Owen Price, George Hall, an unknown vicar and Mr. Kiddall. Front row: Miss Burton, Mrs. Laughton-Smith, Mr. Rushforth (the Mayor), Miss Gwen Price, Reverend Burton, Mrs. Kiddal and Miss Mawer.

69. During the thirties and forties walking was a popular pastime. In those days our roads were free from the articulated lorry, trucks and container traffic. The Louth Rambling Club had been started by Mr. D. Enderby, seen here with his hair parted down the middle and wearing a check pullover (in the centre of the group). The club was to flourish in the years up to the Second World War and still exists to this day.

70. The Girl Guide movement has been long established in Louth. At this gathering in the grounds of the old Kenwick Hall, Mrs. Oscar Dixon was the hostess to Mrs. Tennyson D'Eyncourt of Bayons Manor. This picture was taken in the early thirties at one of the many guide meetings when Mrs. Tennyson D'Eyncourt (seen here standing) gave a speech.

71. H.S. Forman's bakery shop in Upgate was given a new frontage in the 1930's by Mawer Bros. The firm had become well-established and although one of Forman's sons had left the town to start his famous printing works in Nottingham (responsible for printing and producing the Nottingham Evening Post) the bakery continued under the same name. It was bought by Cyril Hanson and continued as a bakery until quite recently.

72. Edmund Allenby was born at Cadwell Hall near Louth. His uncle Captain Allenby of Kenwick Hall (called Kenwick House in those days) was a well-respected local personality and his cousin Henry Charles Hynman Allenby was Lord Lieutenant of the county. So when Edmund Allenby was invited to a dinner held in his honour, the hero of the First World War, friend of Lawrence of Arabia and by now Field Marshall, had no hesitation in accepting. He even signed this card! Seated at the table from left to right are Sir Ernest Sleight, Mrs. Dixon, Field Marshall Sir Edmund Henry Hynman Allenby (1861-1936), Mr. Oscar Dixon, two unknowns, and Lady Sleight.

73. Sadly this is a sight which we shall no longer see – a steam train ploughing its way over Monk's Dyke ridge to Louth Station. The romance of steam trains is one thing, the practicalities of bringing back a rail link to Louth is quite another, but full marks to the Grimsby/Louth Railway Preservation Society who are doing their best to link up the town with the National network once more.

74. A familiar sight to all of us. Two happy shoppers leaving the Wednesday cornmarket, clutching their purchase of vegetables and obviously pleased with their bargain.

THE MARKET PLACE

LOUTH

THE TOWN HALL.

THE MARKET.

ST. JAMES' CHURCH.

EASTGATE.

75. I have included this card (the most recent in the book it dates circa 1950) not because it is a good composite picture, which of course it is but simply because of the publisher. The card was produced by A.V. Fry of London whom I met once in the early 1970's and the firm still trades under the name of Skilton & Fry who publish my own cards of Lincolnshire.

St. James' Church, Louth

76. As another day dawns over Louth the magnificent spire of St. James Church sits quietly and says nothing. As people busy themselves with the hustle and bustle of trade beneath its flying buttresses, the spire remains aloof. Like a silver pencil pointing over the rooftops it just stays silent without breathing a word, but if only that spire could talk, the tales it would tell.